Simon Periton

Masks, Outlaws, Anarchists

There's a romance about knives that no amount of Uzi-culture can undermine – they're so personal, extensions of the hand, Brutus and Caesar, Borges's supernatural gauchos fighting in the night, stilettos and switchblades. Artists, of course, used to think of the palette knife as an essential tool, but their hot-blooded creative temperament meant it wasn't a good idea to give them anything sharper – look what happened to Van Gogh. Simon Periton knows that these hysterical displays belong to another age, and he handles his scalpel with restraint, calm and fastidious, but he can't escape the history. The blade, as a tool, is very different to the charcoal crayon or the badger-hair brush, and there's something unavoidably violent, something Droog-like in the precise and cultured imagery of Periton's work, with its Rorschach-test parade of mirrored psychic symbolism: order and anarchy, imprisonment and escape, love, sex and death; a fashionistic picaresque of links and oppositions as uncomfortably exact as those between the Classical sublime of the great Ludwig van and a sharp kick in the yarbles – if you've got any yarbles.

Periton describes his early works as 'doilies', and the subject of his first adventures in paper-cutting was the collision between the familiar lacy, suburban application of his technique – all Victorian repression and twitching curtains – and the counter-cultural imagery of his patterns, but this simple opposition soon set off a chain of more subtle associations. Elaborating on the initial theme, Periton has invented an idiosyncratic visual language that's literally entwined with the intricate personal mythology it describes, each variation producing a new discovery that feeds back into the procedure of thinking and making. One of the beauties of the method is that its restrictions create a focus, an obligation to learn from the process in order to subvert it. As much as Periton discovers new techniques – reversals of line and void, faked reflection, multiple layering, mutation of one image into another – they discover him. The self-imposed limitations mean that progress takes the form of a kind of fractal expansion, a continual increase in internal complexity, and even recent excursions into three dimensions, substantial feats of cardboard engineering, have maintained the same respect for the basic rules of production.

S.P.   1995   56 x 33 cm / 22 x 21 in
Arts Council Collection, Hayward Gallery, London

Formally, though, despite its technical purity, the work sidesteps Modernist concerns in favour of an older conventionalism. It might be drawing and sculpture – a certain kind of very thin sculpture – both at once. The usefulness of that distinction, like that between medium and support, which Periton also erases faded out some time ago – territory well-charted by Ryman and Fontana among others. More important is the quality of the line, its clean edge, its finality. It has the commitment, and the arcane symbolism, of the tattooist's art. Even as the technique has evolved over time from careful concentration to ambitious craftsmanship, the parameters remain the same – precision, sharp transition, repetition; expression and nuance subordinate to the integrity of the whole design.

The obvious lineage is the conventionalised, pre-Modern tradition of decorative art that comes along with the doily-making process itself, the painstaking symmetries of eighteenth century lacework, the ornamental borders of medieval illumination, the modulated repetitions of Persian weaving. The contradictions between form and content in Periton's doilies seem to update William Morris, whose medievalist approach to tapestry and wallpaper, now a cliché of middle class decor, went hand in hand with revolutionary politics and an activism that led to his rabble-rousing before the 1887 'Bloody Sunday' confrontation in Trafalgar Square. But Periton identifies instead the influence of Morris's foremost contemporary, Christopher Dresser. A Glasgow-born, London-based designer who incorporated Middle Eastern, Asian and Japanese motifs into his wide-ranging production, Dresser produced textiles, wallpaper, ceramics, glassware and metalwork, and decorated his furniture with intricate motifs inspired by Islamic screens.

Beelzebub   2001   28 x 30 cm / 11 x 12 in   Jill Fortunoff, New York

But Dresser's eclectic, proto-functionalist aesthetic marked a point of divergence, the beginning of the industrialisation of the decorative arts, a historical arc with its zenith in the Bauhaus, nadir in IKEA, while Periton's allegiance remains with the Romantic and the Gothic: somewhere, unacknowledged, the ghost of Byron; the trellis-work backdrop to the naked lovers of Aubrey Beardsley's *Mysterious Rose Garden*; the literate, stylised punk of Derek Jarman's early films; Richard Hell's razor-slashed t-shirts and Rimbaud fixation; lace gloves and piercings in mid-seventies Bromley. A line drawn, or sliced, from Goya's *Witches' Sabbath* to Iggy Pop's famously skull-like face half-hidden behind a repeating dodecahedric pattern that suggests a star-filled sky. Eyes are a recurring theme. Eyes, in the cut paper technique, are holes – unavoidably bringing to mind, given Periton's scalpel, the razor blade/eyeball sequence in *Un Chien Andalou*, and, for the connoisseur, the pinned eyelids in Argento's *Opera* and the legendary moment censored (in the UK, if nowhere else) from Fulci's *Zombie Flesh Eaters*. He's made a series of paper bag masks, ritual headgear with sinister overtones in stories from *The Masque of the Red Death* to *The Magus*, the first, with its blind eyes and gaping mouth, a kind of low-budget pink-patterned S&M fetish, sketch for the head of a robot love doll. He's given eyes to a leaf in an image somewhere between Tolkein and Arcimbaldo, and made a staring owl, another mythical symbol of nocturnal ill-luck. At the same time, most of his portraits of people have no eyes, not

Mask (Eyes in the Forest)   1997
44 x 33 x 13 cm / 18 x 13 x 5 in
Collection Sadie Coles

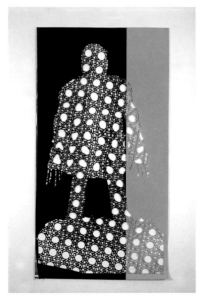

Untitled (Wicker) 2001
300 x 140 cm / 118 x 55 in

even holes, just blank expanses of pattern where the face should be, and the circuit of horror-film reference is completed by *Leatherface* – a portrait of a mask where even the mask is blanked out.

Masks, outlaws, anarchists. The bullet-hole-like burst of *Tunnel* and the Peckinpah-style prison breakout of *Hole in the Wall*. Periton's imagery is born free but is everywhere in chains, or at least ringed with barbed wire, and the holes are not just eyes, but ways out, the Romantic dream recut as a desire for a kind of cultural escape. If the world your art belongs in doesn't exist, it's necessary to signpost the way to it as best you can. All the same, *The Damned* here are frilly-shirted punk cabaret artists Vanian and Scabies, not the lost souls in the inferno, and even *Beelzebub*, Lord of the Flies and so, somehow, patron of Periton's many webs, has rebranded himself, P. Diddy-style, as the *Notorious B.L.Z.* The self-awareness and satirical intent in the humour that runs through the work – from the comic policemen of *Black Riot Fart Doily*, with their camp Keystone poses and elaborately decorated riot shields, to the epic psychosexual snarl-up of *Your War, My Love* – steers it away from sentimentality or revivalism and into a more contemporary kind of mischievous experimentation. The cane-chair pattern first collaged into the history of art by Picasso and Braque is the punchline to *Wickerman*, and Jamie Reid's iconic Sex Pistols logo gets cheekily reworked as Periton's own monogram in *S.P.* The effect of all this is to distance the work both from painterly or religious soul-searching – crowns of thorns, meditations on natural order, the mathematical oneness of the mandala – as well as from the slick, wide-eyed, neo-Modernist shape-throwing of the recent revival in craft and figuration.

Periton doesn't fit easily into any trend or movement. The story of the development of his work is, instead, the story of the opposing ideas thrown together in the beginning – homespun conventionalism vs. punk rock rebellion – not only deconstructing each other, but informing and extending. It's tempting to see this as an autobiographical process, a symbolic re-enactment of conflicting personal influences, resolution or result of early disaffection, but it's more productive to think of it as part of a much longer, popular and intellectual tradition, a disciplined attempt to think about freedom. Right now we're blessed with a stunningly ahistorical media culture that tags the MTV-friendly chirping of Blink 182 as edgy and justifies contemporary art as the research wing of the marketing industry. The ancient tradition of decorative art has been replaced by the constant innovation of technological fashion, and the politicised energy of first-wave punk is soundtrack to the revival of military chic. Given the situation, Periton's work could be an anachronism, but it plays a double game. It might be frail and delicate, materially lightweight – a decent retrospective, properly scrunched, would probably fit in a carrier bag – still it's full of powerful images of oppression and delinquency: the knife that draws the barbs and barricades necessarily the same knife that cuts through them, and the blank-eyed seduction simply a way of drawing you into another web, a new network.

Will Bradley

Barbed Wire Doily 1996
400 x 5 cm / 158 x 2 in

Small Anarchy Doily   1996
51 cm / 21 in diameter

Thorn Doily 1 1996
105 x 70 cm / 41 x 28 in

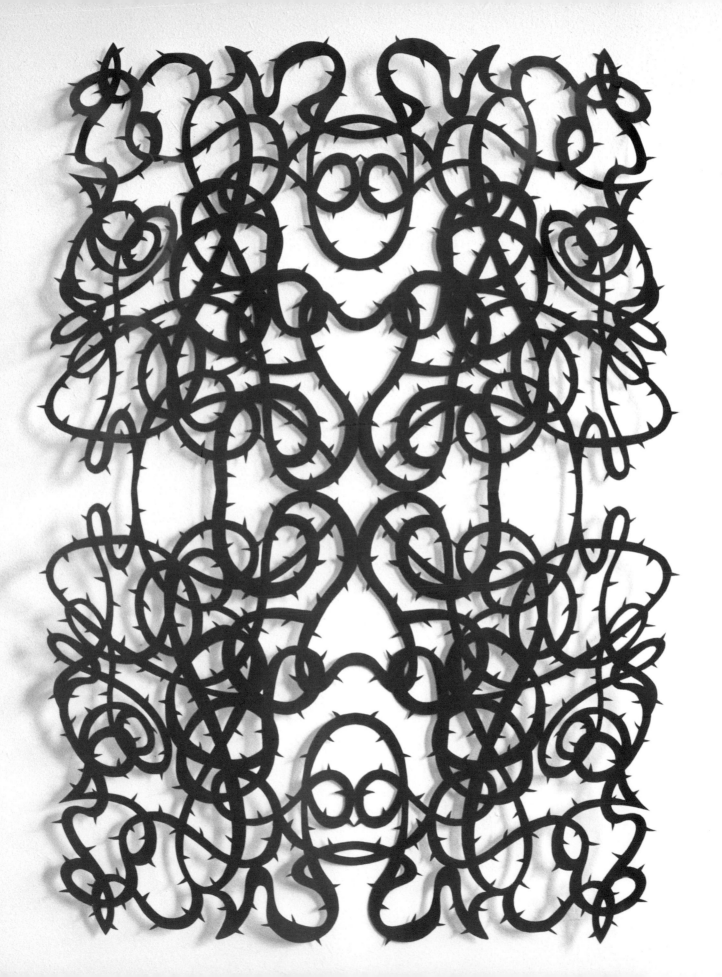

The Hole In the Wall Daily   1996
51 x 76 cm / 20 x 30 in
Destroyed

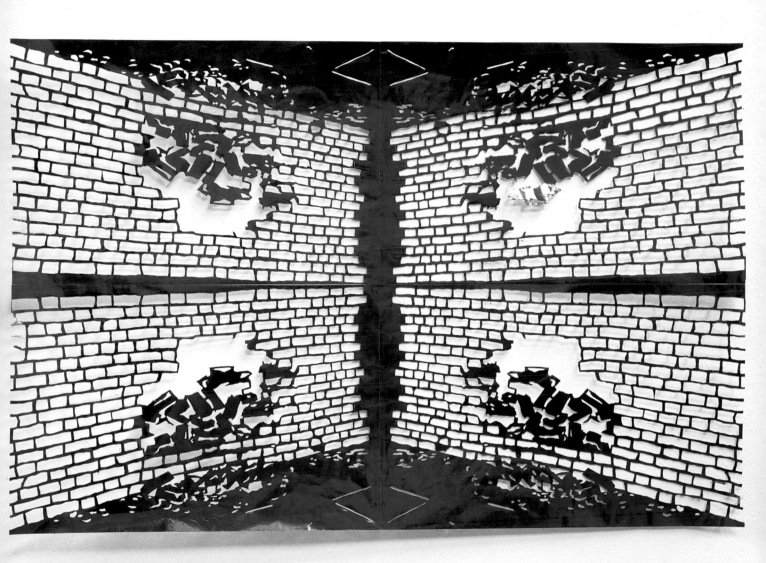

Target Daily with Spikey Farts   1996
122 x 122 cm / 48 x 48 in
Collection Sadie Coles

Your War My Love   1996
840 x 420 cm / 336 x 168 in

Breathless 1998
28 x 31 cm / 11 x 12 in
Unilever plc Contemporary Art Collection

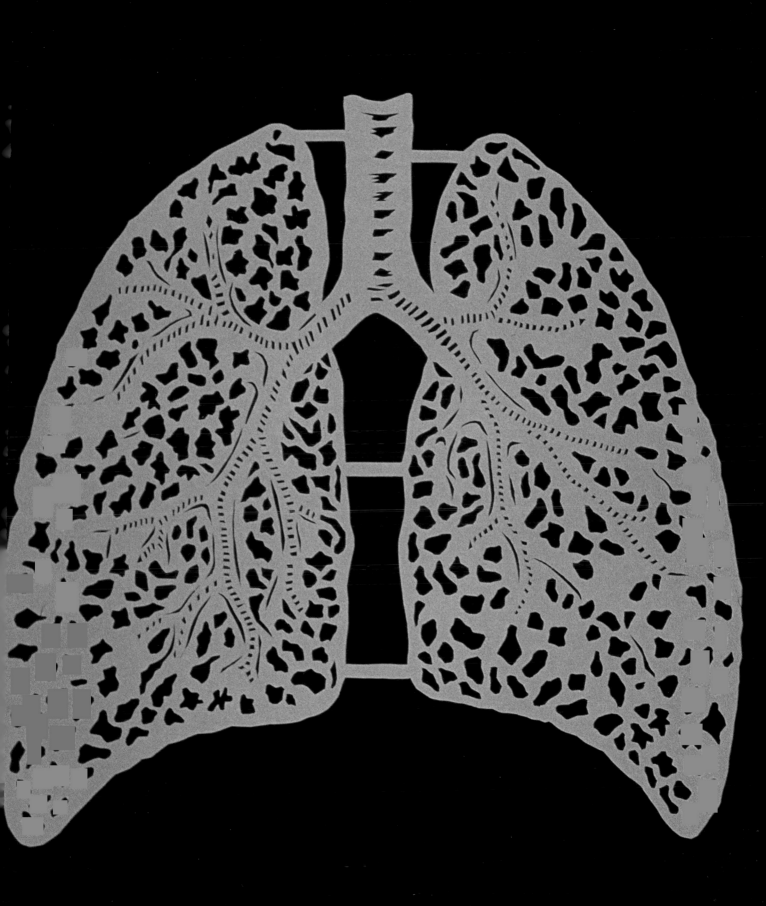

Black Riot Fart Doily   1997
190 cm / 75 in diameter
Städtische Galerie im Lenbachhaus, Munich

Doily for Christopher Dresser 1996
51 x 79 cm / 20 x 31 in
Celebrity Cruises Collection, mv Millennium

Free Radical   1999
178 cm / 70 in diameter

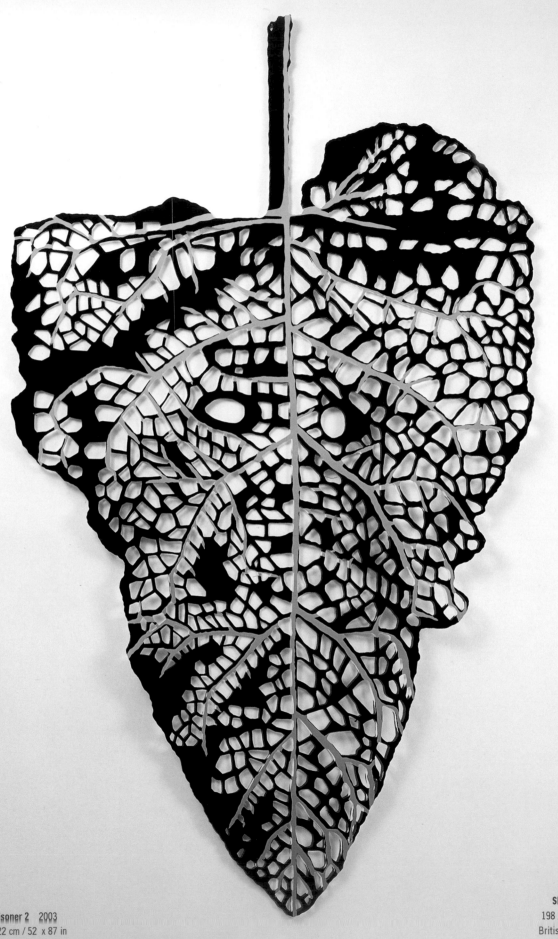

Mint Poisoner 2 2003
131 x 222 cm / 52 x 87 in

Shroud (Iggy) 2001
198 x 49 cm / 78 x 19 in
British Council Collection

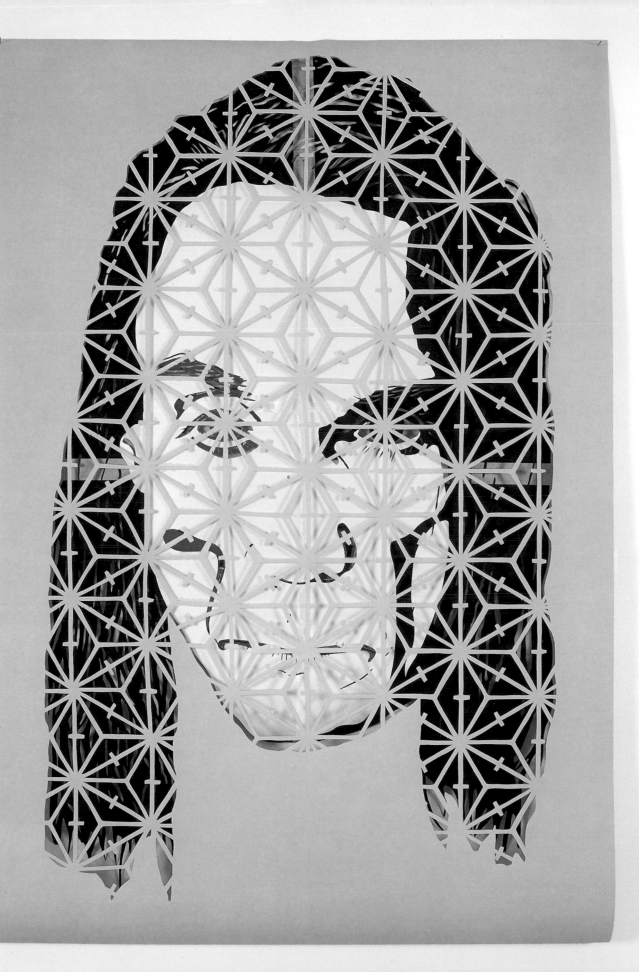

Duchess 2001
198 x 49 cm / 78 x 19 in
Isabella Blow Collection

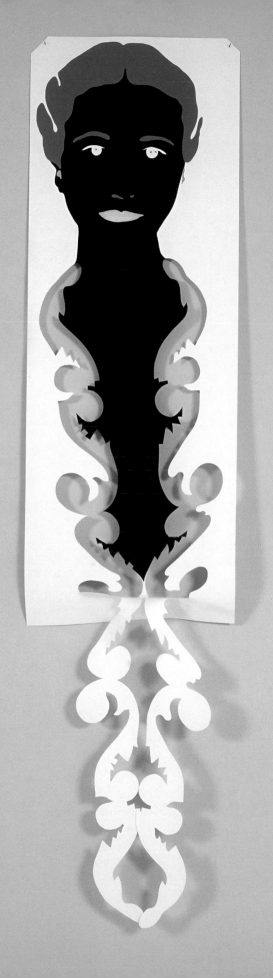

Anne Frank 2002
55 x 50 cm / 22 x 20 in
Collection Patricia Marshall

Double Leather Face   2001
50 x 41 cm / 20 x 16 in
Collection Patricia Marshall

Notorious B.L.Z.   2002
208 x 129 cm / 82 x 51 cm
Lindemann Collection, Miami Beach, Florida

Domestic Violence   2001
triptych, each: 69 x 53 cm / 27 x 20 in
Collection Andrew & Stephanie Hale

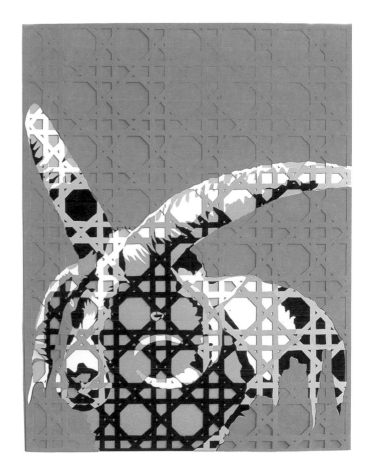

Jayne II   2002
74 x 61 cm / 29 x 24 in
Collection of David Harry Stewart, New York

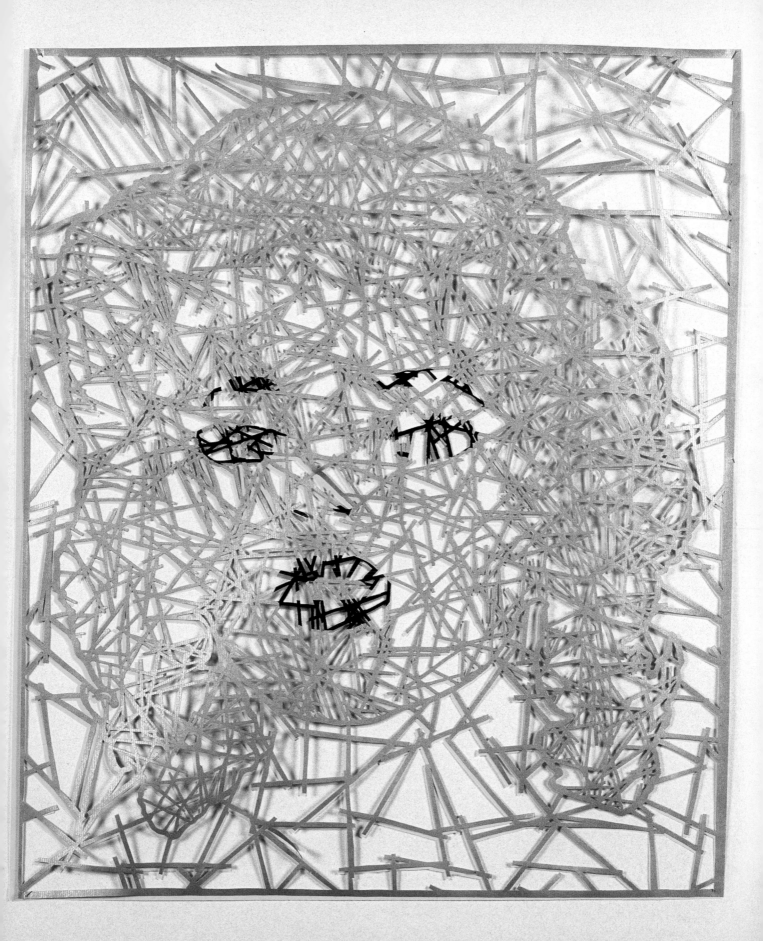

Charger 2003
278 mm / 110 in diameter
The West Collection at SEI

Gate 2003
218 x 124 cm / 86 x 49 in

The Damned 2001
132 x 120 cm / 52 x 48 in

X Flag 2003
224 x 124 cm / 88 x 49 in

Lantern 2 2003
160 x 152 cm / 63 x 60 in

Scalpels 1999